# SUCCESSFUL TENNIS

## 303 TIPS

# SUCCESSFUL TENNIS

## 303 TIPS

Angela Buxton and Nenad Simic

FIREFLY BOOKS

# A FIREFLY BOOK

Published by Firefly Books Ltd. 2010
Copyright © 2010 A & C Black Publishers Ltd.

First Printing

**Publisher Cataloging-in-Publication Data (U.S.)**

Buxton, Angela.
     Successful tennis : 303 tips /
Angela Buxton and Nenad Simic.
[   ] p. : col. photos.  ;  cm.
Summary: A training manual with short tips and advice on the forehand, volley, serve and mental game.
ISBN-13: 978-1-55407-663-5 (pbk.)
ISBN-10: 1-55407-663-3 (pbk.)
1. Tennis. I. Simic, Nenad. II. Title.
796.342 dc22     GV995.B89     2010

**Library and Archives Canada Cataloguing in Publication**

Buxton, Angela, 1934-
     Successful tennis : 303 tips /
Angela Buxton and Nenad Simic.
ISBN-13: 978-1-55407-663-5 (pbk.)
ISBN-10: 1-55407-663-3 (pbk.)
     1. Tennis. I. Simic, Nenad II. Title. III. Title: Successful tennis and three hundred and three tips.
GV995.B89 2010    796.342'2 C2010900121-4

Published in the United States by
Firefly Books (U.S.) Inc.
P.O. Box 1338, Ellicott Station
Buffalo, New York  14205

Published in Canada by
Firefly Books Ltd.
66 Leek Crescent
Richmond Hill, Ontario  L4B 1H1

Printed in China

**Photo Credits**
Cover photographs © Shutterstock (top); © PA Photos (bottom)
Inside photographs © PA Photos 13, 17, 18, 25, 40, 42, 49, 52, 54, 57, 70, 73, 81, 84; © Shutterstock 21, 33, 36, 61, 85, 96; © Nenad Simic 11, 30, 92; © Angela Buxton 53.

**Note**
While every effort has been made to ensure that the content of this book is as technically accurate and as sound as possible, neither the author nor the publishers can accept responsibility for any injury or loss sustained as a result of the use of this material.

# CONTENTS

## Dedication

This book is dedicated to my two children Marta and Filip, who together with my wife Jasna gave me both the time and the inspiration to write this book.

One evening, following an argument with my wife, I took refuge in our spare room. In a foul mood, I sat down at my computer in the corner of the room and wondered how to calm myself down.

I had been thinking about writing this book for a few years, but I was always short of time. Unable to sleep that night, the ideas began to form in my mind . . . and then on the computer. That night I wrote and wrote.

Next morning I felt much better — and I had something to show for such a silly row! I believe I should thank my wife Jasna once again for creating the situation for this to happen!

# FOREWORD

Nenad is one of the few people I know who is as passionate about tennis as I am. His knowledge knows no bounds, particularly when it comes to the Serbian stars of today.

One day Nesa (as he is affectionately known in the tennis world) told me about a book of 303 tips and ideas he had written for competitive Serbian tennis players to carry with them to competitions. Unfortunately it was only in circulation in Serbian, in Serbia! I thought it was a great idea for serious players to have a small, succinct reference book at hand, especially when they got into trouble during a match, and I wondered why no one else had ever thought of it before.

So when Nesa approached me to rewrite and expand the idea into English for English-speaking players, I jumped at the opportunity.

A five minute read while traveling to matches, in rain delays or at set-all when your opponent inconveniently goes off for a washroom break, could help turn a disadvantage into an advantage. This book is a great memory jogger — enforcing the important details that can convert losing into winning. My advice? Never leave this book at home!

Lastly, my thanks go to Isaac Waterman and Goran Jankovic for helping with the initial translation.

**Angela Buxton**

P.S. Remember, your tennis bag is the right place for this book — not the bookshelf!

# INTRODUCTION

This book is written for players who plan to participate at a competitive level and for those who are already doing so. I have left the basics of the game to others. The 303 tips and ideas will be of the most use to people who take their tennis seriously — be it at competition and tournament level or at a hard-fought weekly match between friends.

Most of the advice given here is a result of my personal experience of coaching over the last twenty years in clubs and academies across the world, from Serbia to Florida. A few of the tips are from anonymous tennis professionals, coaches and tennis fans who just wanted to let everyone know about their experiences and share their knowledge.

As you may know, any form of competitive tennis is a battle. Of course part of this battle can be *fun*, but the goal must always be to win! The tips in this book are written in as informal a way as possible, meaning you can dip in and quickly grasp the idea — especially invaluable in the sections which might come in handy during a match.

I just wish I had started to write all this down earlier. I would have remembered so much more!

**Nenad Simic**

# Tips to
# Improve
# your Forehand

**GRIP/STANCE:** The more extreme the grip, the more open your forehand stance needs to be.

**EARLY PREPARATION:** Whenever you can, prepare your forehand while your opponent's ball is still in the air.

**GOOD FOLLOW-THROUGH IS ESSENTIAL:** To improve your forehand, make sure the racket handle is high on the left side (for right-handers) with the butt facing your opponent.

Serbian Nina Pantic demonstrates the high follow-through, clearly showing the butt of the racket facing her opponent.

To practice the movement so your racket hand ends up across your body on the opposite shoulder, finish the stroke off as if you were listening to a watch ticking on that wrist!

Alternatively, practice catching the racket with your spare hand.

**WEIGHT TRANSFERENCE:** To improve the power in this shot, transfer your weight from the back/right foot (for right-handers) to the front/left foot by using good hip and shoulder rotation.

**INSIDE-OUT FOREHAND:** Regularly practice this shot into your opponent's backhand-side. This can really work when a short ball pitches in the middle of your court. Be ready to attack it.

Similarly you left-handed players need to practice your "inside-out" forehands from the deuce court; always aiming to place the ball deep into your opponent's backhand wing — assuming it is their weakest wing. This exercise also improves your footwork as most of the time it means moving around the ball with little steps in order to attack it with your strong forehand.

**OPEN STANCE:** If you prefer an open stance, your shoulders will control the shot, not your hand or wrist. Learn to rotate your upper body and swing towards the target.

Elena Dementieva of Russia prepares for a powerful smash, with her arm well away from her body.

**USE OF MUSCLE GROUPS IN LEGS, BACK AND SHOULDERS:** When you use the "open-stance" forehand be sure to engage the large muscle groups in your legs, lower back and shoulders, which will result in a better shot. Whether you choose the "closed" or "open" stance, make sure your body is *never* parallel to the sidelines.

**THE POWER OF THE CONTACT ZONE:** The contact zone is just before and just after contact with the ball is made. The faster and more deliberately you can swing through the contact zone, the more powerful your shot will become.

To increase your racket-head speed through the contact zone try using a heavier racket for a short while. Alternatively you can experiment by placing light weights at the head of your racket with lead tape (wide sticky tape, easily available from specialty tennis shops).

Keep your playing arm away from your body — you will produce a more powerful shot.

**THE POWER OF PLAYING DEEP:** If your hardest, most powerful ball is short, or even in the middle of the court, it is never as effective as a deeply struck ball. Hard and deep is the ultimate goal.

**USE OF TARGETS:** Place targets deep into the court, near your opponent's baseline, and practice your forehand by trying to hit them.

In order to improve your explosiveness on your forehand, practice for a short while without the ball but with your racket-head cover on. After a while, still with the cover on, try hitting the ball. Finally, notice how easy it is when you take the cover off.

**DEALING WITH LOW, SHORT BALLS:** In order to produce the best result from low, short balls, add a little hop onto your front foot, bend, then follow through low in a crouched position. Finish the drill by going forward to take up a net position.

**INCREASING THE AGGRESSION ON YOUR FOREHAND:** Try to hit the ball a fraction earlier, while the ball is still on the rise.

**DEALING WITH HIGH-BOUNCING BALLS:** Take the ball slightly in front of your body, with a follow-through behind the opposite hip.

**PRACTICING ACCURACY:** One excellent way to practice forehand accuracy is to rally only in the doubles alley.

**THE FOREHAND TOPSPIN LOB:** When you practice this difficult shot, make sure the follow-through is *above* your racket shoulder. Try practicing with both hands on the racket — this improves the follow-through. If you are a naturally two-handed player try to perfect this shot, particularly the short-cross variety.

# Tips to
# Improve
# your Backhand

**STANCE:** In a good backhand stance, the opponent should be able to view your back.

Russian player Mikhail Youzhny clearly demonstrates the one-handed backhand with his back to his opponent while preparing to strike the ball.

**KNEES:** Your knees should be bent as if just getting up from a chair.

THE ONE-HANDED BACKHAND
**WRIST AND FOLLOW-THROUGH:** A good one-handed backhand is characterized by a firm wrist and follow-through while your spare hand is extended backwards, helping you to balance.

Practice throwing a frisbee. This is the exact action you need to copy, especially when the weight is transferred forward to your front foot on the follow-through. Get it right and you should have the perfect one-handed backhand!

**PLAYING DOWN THE LINE:** When you're playing this shot with a one-handed backhand, remember to hit the ball a little later than you would if you were hitting cross-court.

**HIPS:** When you're aiming down the line don't turn or open your hips too soon — this may lead to hitting the ball toward the middle of the court.

**SHOULDER:** Always aim at your target with your shoulder.

**LOB:** The one-handed backhand lob is similar to the forehand lob using the normal eastern grip. If successful, your next move is toward the net.

**ARM EXTENSION:** Your playing arm should be fully extended otherwise your wrist comes into play. This means you're less in control.

**BACKSWING:** Your backswing needs to accelerate gradually so that you are at top speed when you make contact with the ball.

**ROTATING YOUR BODY:** Try not to think too much about your backswing. Focus instead on ball contact and rotating your body. This will help you bring your racket to the right position. This is the same for both one-handed and two-handed backhands.

## THE TWO-HANDED BACKHAND
**USE OF SPARE HAND:** Think of this shot as a forehand played with your weaker hand. So for right-handed players it can be practiced as a left-handed forehand.

**THE GRIP:** Your dominant hand should use the eastern (shake-hands) or continental grip. Your non-dominant hand should apply the semi-western.

**THE NON-DOMINANT HAND:** This is the hand that leads the racket for the two-handed backhand.

**THE WEAKER HAND:** Surprisingly your weaker hand produces the power. Your dominant hand provides the topspin.

**HANDS TOGETHER OR APART?** Some players like to have their hands a little apart on the grip, stressing the role of the weaker hand. Experiment to find out what works for you.

Viktor Troicki of Serbia uses the two-handed backhand with an eastern grip. He allows a little space between his hands.

**THE FOLLOW-THROUGH:** After the follow-through, your left shoulder (for right-handed players) should be underneath your chin and the racket head should be touching your back. The reverse is true for left-handed players.

**SHOULDERS:** Your shoulders should help you aim. Try not to focus too much on your arms — this tends to impede wrist movement and can make your shots inaccurate.

**THE TWO-HANDED BACKHAND LOB:** This topspin lob is usually pretty effective because it is difficult for your opponent to read. Preparation and swing are similar to the ground stroke, but the face of your racket is slightly more open and the movement is upward.

**STROKE PLAY**
**SLICE:** To slice a backhand, think about knifing the ball downward with underspin.

Practicing underspin: in a standing position use the backhand side of the racket face and keep bouncing the ball up in the air in a left to right movement, applying more and more underspin as you control the flight of the ball. Whether you're practicing this shot in a standing position or actually playing it on the court, try to keep the ball on the strings as long as possible.

**DROP-SHOT:** Applying a little slice here pays dividends because the ball dies more quickly. The drop-shot (identical for both forehand and backhand) should always be a surprise shot and you can play it either in front or diagonally. The shot in front is slightly better as the ball is in the air for less time, so your opponent has less time to see it and react!

**BACKHAND SLICE APPROACH TO NET:** This is usually the best approach shot as it stays low, which means in order to pass you at the net, your opponent has to hit *up* on the ball, making it much easier for you to volley.

**TOPSPIN:** Practice the topspin backhand with a training partner. While your partner is hitting with underspin you can work on your topspin. This way you both get something out of a practice session!

**LOBBING FLAT OR WITH UNDERSPIN:** Use this only as a last resort. If it is successful your next move should be toward the net, exactly the same as the topspin lob.

**RETURNING A HIGH-BOUNCING BALL:** Give this shot more room than usual, whether you're hitting with one hand or two. The idea is to create more space for the follow-through.

**BACKHAND WEAKER SHOT?** Although the backhand is the more natural shot of the two ground strokes, if it is the weaker one for you try not to over hit. Just aim to keep the ball in play and try a little under-spin for extra control. Wait for the opportunity to run around and smack a forehand instead and this way you can apply more speed and strength.

# Tips to
# Improve
# your Serve

**THROWING THE BALL:** In the early stages of learning to serve, practice throwing the ball across the net with the playing hand (like a baseball pitcher). This is a quick way to figure out the correct, easy flowing action you'll need. Then swap the ball for a racket. Place the ball in the throwing hand and try to coordinate both hands together.

**HELP WITH THE BALL TOSS:** It might be useful to have your coach place the ball in the air for you — this really helps if you're having difficulty coordinating, as many players do at first. It will also help to build your confidence — with an accurate placing up of the ball you will be much quicker to make contact.

**THE GRIP:** The most recommended grip is the continental. This is halfway between the eastern forehand and the backhand. Here the fingers are spread out so that the leather grip of the racket is visible through the fingers. This releases your wrist in order to be able to snap at the ball later in the action.

**TOSSING INCORRECTLY:** Never hit a poorly tossed ball! Just catch the ball and start again. Remember, there is nothing in the rules that penalizes a player for doing this, provided no actual attempt has been made to hit the ball beforehand.

**HEAD AND EYES UP!** Make sure that when you make contact with the ball your eyes are looking at the ball. The best way to do this is by keeping your head *up* until the point of contact.

**TOSSING ARM UP!** One of the best kept secrets of a good service action is to make sure your tossing arm stays as high as possible in contact with the ball. Place the ball in the air at the last possible moment. Remember that the hand holding the ball moves into action first.

Ways to practice the toss
**a** To help your tossing arm stay up and not descend too quickly, try clicking your fingers at the height of the ball toss, once the ball has been released and before the actual strike.

**b** Place a racket-head cover in front of your left big toe (for right-handers). Now without actually hitting the ball, toss the ball up as accurately as possible with the tossing hand, as described above, and let it drop — hopefully on the racket-head cover. This is called half-serve practice.

**c** When you are practicing your toss try and imagine placing the ball at its peak in a basketball hoop.

**RITUALS:** Whether you're in a practice or match situation try to maintain the same rituals. For you this might involve bouncing the ball, rocking, or just pausing while your mind clears and you collect your thoughts.

**EYES CLOSED:** Sometimes it is helpful to practice serving with your eyes closed. This can help perfect your tossing action while preventing you from looking too soon to see where the serve has landed.

**FIRST SERVE IN:** In matches, aim to make your first serve percentage at least 60 percent. Try playing practice matches using only one ball to serve — this can really help to improve your first serve percentage!

**KEYWORD:** Think of a keyword like "yes!" or "ace!" or "boom!" when you make contact with the ball — it can really help to focus your concentration.

**KNEELING:** It might sound odd, but try practicing serving while you're kneeling on a towel. Start with the racket already way back, well away from your body in the throwing position, and remember to hit *up*. If this is done correctly it can generally really help your shoulder and body rotation.

**BREATHING:** Calm your breathing with a few deep breaths before you serve — especially after a long point. Learn to listen to your breathing. Do this when you are toweling down or collecting a ball. It doesn't take long and can make all the difference.

**IN THE WARM-UP:** Use the warm-up to practice some deep second serves until you feel your shoulder is warmed up and you have gained some confidence.

**ADDING POWER TO YOUR SERVE:** Bend your knees prior to making contact. After tossing the ball, do not rush to hit it and lose your rhythm. Remember to hold the racket back as far as possible from your body, bending up your wrist, as if you are opening a bow and arrow. Keep it slow at this stage and only turn your wrist over at the last possible second. Finally, accelerate into the hitting zone with a "snap" of your wrist.

**SERVING WIDE:** If you want to serve wide you need to add some slice. Try to position your feet slightly farther away from the center mark on the baseline and remember to be subtle about it — your opponent might well be on the look-out for clues.

Mix up your serves
a Serve a second serve first, or instead of a second serve, risk a more powerful first serve in its place.

**b.** Vary the placement and speed of the ball — two variables at your disposal when you are serving. Remember, it is *always* a good strategy to keep your opponent guessing!

**FOOT-FAULT:** You need to get as much out of your serve as possible without foot-faulting. During the action your knees, hips and shoulders need to become heavily engaged. In fact when you lean in to hit the ball, it might seem as if they are over the baseline, however this is OK provided neither foot crosses over the baseline before you make contact with the ball.

Marta Simic, serving with both feet well behind the baseline, but knees, hips and shoulders hanging well over the baseline, giving her an advantage.

**SERVE AND VOLLEY:** This is a good tactic to use occasionally, in order to keep your opponent guessing and on their toes.

**PRACTICING SERVE AND VOLLEY:** Try to throw the ball as far forward as possible and explore how far you can actually reach without foot-faulting.

**SECOND SERVE BEING ATTACKED?** If your opponent is successfully attacking your second serve, try and slice your second serve wide.

**BODY SERVE:** To keep your opponent honest try to "jam" the serve by using some slice, so that when the ball bounces it swerves into the body.

**KICK SERVE TO THE BACKHAND:** This is a good serve to use, particularly against single-handed backhand players. The high kick usually causes them difficulties!

**ACCELERATE THE FOLLOW-THROUGH:** Don't allow your follow-through to slow down, especially on second serves.

**SHADOW AND SING:** When you're practicing your serve, or during matches in between points, it's good for your shoulder if you "shadow" a few serves, just with the racket. It might sound strange, but quietly sing or hum a little song to yourself while you're doing it — you'll be amazed at how much calmer you feel.

## CREATE CONFIDENCE IN YOUR SERVE:
During a critical phase in the match — and particularly after double-faulting — have the confidence to go for an ace. Most players just want to get their first serve in on the next point, but champions always go for the ace. This really throws the opposition off balance as they are expecting something weaker. Remember — this confidence is the difference between a champion's mentality and a loser's.

# Tips to
# Improve your
# Return of Serve

**ENVISION:** Before the point starts envision how you might return. This will also help you concentrate.

**RECOGNITION OF YOUR STRENGTHS:** Learn to recognize where your strengths lie. For example, Agassi liked to take control of the point immediately with his return, whereas Sampras preferred to return deep into the court and look for his opportunity as the point played out. Understanding this will help a lot in your return of serve strategy.

**POSITION OF READINESS:** Use the grip with which you are most comfortable. Never be afraid to experiment to find what works best for you.

### Planning

**a** Before the point starts decide whether you plan to rush the net, stay back or play a drop shot, if given the opportunity.

**b** Then choose whether just to block the serve back, or hit the ball with underspin or topspin, etc.

**SPLIT-STEP:** Whatever you decide to do, make a split-step (a hop with both feet) just before your opponent serves.

## Never retreat

a Never ever take a step back when returning serve.

b However, if you're faced with a very powerful server you might choose to take up your stance well behind the baseline *beforehand*, in order to give you more time to see the ball.

**ANTICIPATION:** The few seconds before the server delivers his serve are vitally important. During this short space of time you can pick up valuable clues which you can immediately use to your advantage. Watch in case your opponent's stance changes. Their toss, position of their shoulders and hips can all give away what they're intending to do. For example, if the server tosses the ball more to their right, this is likely to result in a "sliced serve." If the ball toss is more over the head the result will probably be a topspin serve.

**PATIENCE:** Never lose patience or get upset when your opponent makes a few winning serves. Remind yourself that you're bound to get several opportunities on their second serves.

**USING YOUR 20 SECONDS:** If you make a few unsuccessful returns, don't give up! Use your allotted 20 seconds between points to use your towel, adjust your strings or tie your shoelaces, while you think about a change to your strategy. Remember, this is all within

Venus Williams takes an aggressive, intensely-focused return of serve position.

the rules of the game — even if the server is waiting for you.

**KEYWORD:** When you're hitting a return select a positive key word or phrase to say like "yes!" or "right!" or "hit it!" or "I can!"

## INCREASING YOUR CONCENTRATION: As
this is "invisible" it is a very useful ploy to use. It also
relieves mental pressure as the match progresses.

## WHEN TO START AIMING FOR THE LINES:
Think about placing the ball closer to the lines only when
you feel comfortable returning your opponent's serves.

## USE YOUR FOREHAND RETURN MORE: Try
and make more returns with your forehand. This probably means moving your feet more sometimes, in order
to get around the ball, but most players are more
successful on their forehand.

## CONSISTENCY OF RETURNS: Winning tennis
matches is all about consistency, so make sure your
percentage of returns is as high as possible, even if they
land mid-court. The controlled, wide return of serve is
the high percentage return, because there is the most
room across the court. Remember, your chance to actually win the point usually comes later.

## THE ADVANTAGE OF LEANING INTO THE
BALL: Remember to always lean forward into the ball
on return. Make this a habit and you'll find you have
improved balance and better contact with the ball.

**TWO-HANDED BACKHANDERS:** If you're short of time, roll your wrist behind your racket, shorten the swing and use more of your wrist than usual. Then step into your shot with your front foot.

## INTIMIDATION

**a** If you manage to hit a few outright winners off your opponent's second serve you will intimidate them and put extra pressure on their first serve in the future. This extra pressure very often results in double-faults later on.

**b** Another trick is to stand well inside the baseline so that the server notices that you have changed your position. This adds extra pressure for them to come up with something even better than before, often resulting in double-faults for them and extra confidence for you. Be warned though that this tactic needs to be well rehearsed and practiced, because the timing of the return is much faster.

## SPEEDING UP REACTIONS

**a** To practice the different timing required when you stand inside the baseline, have a friend or coach serve hard at you from well inside their baseline.

**b** Another way to speed up your reactions is to shorten your backswing. Simply avoid using the full backswing, and aim to get your racket back in position earlier.

## SHORTENING YOUR BACKSWING:

a Have your coach serve 30 or so balls to you from inside their baseline while you simply lean on the return and rush the net. This will improve your ball contact and control. Or try this practice — the server tells you where they intend to serve, and all you have to do is place your racket back even before the ball crosses the net and just follow through.

b The above ideas will really help in a match when you're faced with powerful servers and they will also help you block back serves effectively. This is something that you need to learn sooner or later when you're facing big servers. Building your confidence in this way also relieves a lot of mental pressure in big matches.

## ATTACKING SECOND SERVES: Always be on
the alert to attack any weak second serves. Aim to run around the ball and attack it with your stronger wing, usually the forehand. Keep your feet wide and stay low when you're hitting.

## BLUFFING: A great tactic — every now and then
deliberately leave one side of the service box open. When the server is committed (having already tossed the ball) move back in position and cover the opening.

**PLAYING A NET RUSHER:** Make sure your return is low and use some topspin if possible. It is much more difficult for an incoming volleyer to return a dipping ball which has topspin. They have to then volley up, giving you a good opportunity for the pass on your second shot.

**THE DROP SHOT:** This is not usually advisable as it's a risky strategy unless you're facing an opponent who obviously dislikes the net position or who is a slow mover.

Jelena Jankovic plays a forehand volley with the head of the racket laid slightly back to elevate the ball over the net.

**IN CRITICAL MOMENTS:** Try to move forward and hit your return properly. Try shadowing the stroke in the few seconds beforehand. Use a sequence of strokes following your return that you know works for you. Try to resist the temptation to just gently push the ball over the net.

**PLAY DOUBLES!** Playing doubles helps speed up your reaction for the low cross-court return. It also helps improve your balance and accuracy. A highly recommended addition to your training!

# Tips to
# Improve your
# Footwork

## GOOD TECHNIQUE WITHOUT FOOTWORK?

If your aim is to win tennis matches, however good your technique is, without good footwork, it isn't much use.

**FOOTWEAR:** Make sure you wear the appropriate footwear for the surface you're playing on — clay shoes enable you to slide better, and hard and grass shoes help prevent you from sliding at all. This will all help your footwork and prevent injuries.

## WEIGHT

**a** To produce your best results you need to be at your optimum playing weight. Consult with a dietician, and then, in discussion with your coach, aim to reach and *stay* at that weight. Even a little bit of weight gain will make your footwork suffer.

**b** To improve your balance when you're playing, your weight needs to be on the balls of your feet.

**PREPARATION:** The prerequisite for a good stroke is good preparation. This means ample shoulder rotation, early backswing and generous footwork. Remember that the key is always to reach the ball with time to spare. This can only happen with efficient footwork.

## WAYS TO IMPROVE

**a** Do at least two "potato races" per day with four balls, increasing to six over time with 15 seconds in between. See Figure 1.

Balls are distributed at equal distances along a line with the runner collecting the furthest ball before running back to the start each time, until all the balls are collected.

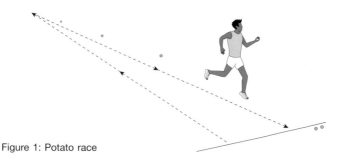

Figure 1: Potato race

**b** Ideally practice with two or more players, all racing against each other, to increase your speed; this drill can also be done alone with good results. Use tennis balls instead of potatoes — they're more accessible during a practice session!

**c** Line up the balls in a straight line, about 3 to 4 feet (1–1.2 meters) apart. Run and collect each one separately, carefully placing it back in the start position, which can be marked by an empty box, or merely by a chalked line. The order in which you pick up the balls doesn't matter at all because the same distance is covered in the lon

e Be sure to practice running down both sides of the line of balls, to develop a quick turn on both sides.

f These races really help movement, because of the intensity of the constant bending and turning, and the short, sharp sprints.

**SKIPPING ROPE:** Fast skipping is best! Pass the rope under the feet *twice* to each jump. Keep your knees as high as possible and skip with as much variation as possible — the more showing off the better! For example, swing the rope sideways in between jumps, introduce a little backward skipping and so on. This helps a lot with motivation and stops the practice getting boring. Practice skipping every day if you can. Skipping can also be used as a beneficial warm-up before matches, particularly if there is no practice court available. The great thing about skipping is that it can be done anywhere and anytime — even in a hotel room!

**SLALOM RACES:** This is a great practice to perfect the small side steps which you need so often to return wide balls. Set up some cones a few feet away from one another and practice weaving in and out, preferably against other players. Or work alone and time yourself against the clock, constantly working to improve your timing.

**STEP-TRAINING:** Simply use any staircase to improve footwork and general agility. You can do this on your own, using a clock to work to improve your time over 20, 30, 40 or even 50 steps up and down.

**MINI-HURDLE TRAINING:** Mini-hurdles are useful for general agility. Remember to keep the knees high.

**PLAY MINI-TENNIS:** Try playing mini-tennis using *flat* balls! The balls don't bounce as high, so more bending and better footwork is required.

**SHORT OF TIME? WIDE BALL?**
**a** Try to pivot on the foot closest to the ball. Good foot-work comes into play because without it, this isn't very effective.

**b** After hitting a wide ball on the stretch, try for a faster recovery shot by pushing off with the outside foot. Then use a cross-over step, passing one foot over the other. Finally, start running with cross-over steps to the middle of the court.

**KEEP MOVING:** Don't wait for the ball to cross the net before you move your feet. Keep your feet moving all the time, anticipating your opponent's shot, and envision what footwork will be needed.

**QUICKEN YOUR RECOVERY:** Practice an open or semi-open stance for both forehand and backhand strokes — this helps the feet to cover the court better and means a faster recovery.

**AVOID LONG, LATERAL MOVEMENTS:** You will find it harder to change direction or recover quickly. Use them only for the first one or two steps if necessary.

**DEFENDING FROM THE CORNERS OF THE COURT?** In these circumstances it is best to use the open stance for either the forehand or two-handed backhand. Lean against the outside foot. Then make a "hop-step" with that foot to balance yourself. The "hop-step" will also give you a speedier recovery toward the middle of the court and eliminate additional steps.

**LATE FOR THE BALL?** Simply turn your shoulders and sprint to the ball. Hit it whichever way you can. Don't think about it too much. Allow your subconscious and your speed-training to take over.

**ATTACKING A SHORTER BALL:** If you have ample time, or even better if you find yourself a few steps inside the baseline, approach the ball with a semi-open or open stance, transferring your weight from your back to your front foot with small steps while rotating your hips.

**ENDURED A LONG POINT?** If you have just completed a long, energy-sapping point and won, it sends a clear message to your opponent that you have sound footwork and that you are mentally and physically fit. This is worth two points anytime!

**OUT OF BREATH?** However if you are still out of breath and need time to recover, use your 20 seconds between points to take a breather. Use your towel, change your racket or tie your shoelaces.

**PLAYING AN EXPERIENCED PLAYER:** An experienced player will usually surprise you by returning a few more balls than most. Don't underestimate their footwork ability. Even though the point may look like it has ended in your favor, expect the ball to come back one more time. Keep your feet moving in the direction of the ball at all times and don't get taken by surprise!

# Tips to
# Improve
# your Volley

THE CLASSICAL VOLLEY
**STANCE/TOES:** The best volleys are usually played on your toes, rather than flat-footed.

**PUNCH YOUR VOLLEYS:** Classical volleys are always punched. *Never* swing at them.

**THE VOLLEY MOTION:** Although this is a simple punching of the ball, it is also similar in motion to knocking on a door.

**THE GRIP:** The most effective grip to use is the continental for both forehand and backhand. This is similar to the service grip but not as far around to the left, and the fingers are not as spread out as in the serve.

**STANCE/HIGH HOLD:** Have a high hold across the body with your racket head always higher than your wrist. For classical volleys, when you take up your position of readiness (when your partner is serving, for example) the racket should be held at shoulder height so that when contact is made you are ready to simply lean on the ball and punch it away. Otherwise it would be necessary to make two movements — bringing the racket up, then punching the ball.

**THE WRIST:** Unlike other strokes in tennis where you use your wrist, when hitting a classical volley your wrist should be firm and braced.

**FEET:** The hidden power behind the explosive volley is in pushing off with the correct foot. If the time is available, push off with your right foot for the forehand volley as you lean on the ball, landing on your left foot (for right-handers). The opposite is true for the classical backhand volley.

**STRAIGHT ARM:** If possible try to volley with a straight arm, both forehand and backhand.

**CONTACT IN FRONT:** You will see the ball much better if you make contact in front of your body.

**HIGH BALLS:** When you are faced with a high ball, keep your racket in front of your body and step into the shot. Your body, not your arm, will supply the power.

**EYES:** Your eyes should be glued to the ball at all times. When you're making a volley commit yourself to the ball. Never let the ball "play" you! And certainly never look at the opponent when volleying.

**TWO-HANDED BACKHAND VOLLEYS:** This is a good volley for balls close to the body. For wide volleys let go with one hand when you have to reach wide. Always have the correct grip so that you can switch quickly to support the one hand.

## HALF-VOLLEYS

**a** This is one of the most difficult shots in the game and should be avoided if at all possible. It usually means that you are standing in the wrong position i.e., too far back in no man's land. If you want to familiarize yourself with this difficult volley, which does appear from time to time, play a lot of doubles!

Here, Jarkko Nieminen of Finland plays a one-handed shot as he approaches the net. On this type of shot, when the ball is low, it is always advisable to play w  one hand only.

b After hitting a half-volley make a habit of always advancing quickly to the net for an easier next shot.

**STAND CLOSE TO THE NET:** Standing closer to the net when playing classical volleys gives you better angles and reach. You are also able to impose yourself and your game better from this position.

**AFRAID TO VOLLEY?** If you have trouble volleying or have weak wrists, try holding the racket up the neck with three fingers spread out on the strings and secured at the back with the thumb (see below).

When you practice this it is important that the racket shaft should run straight down your arm to act as a brace for your wrist. Don't let the racket shaft swing to either side of your arm, otherwise the brace effect is immediately lost.

If you have difficulty volleying, try this "3-finger hold." Make sure the shaft of your racket runs down your arm to steady and control your hit.

**VOLLEY ON THE RUN:** Make sure that when moving forward to the ball, you keep the racket head steady. Do not allow the racket head to drop down on making contact.

**BETTER CONTROL:** For better control of your forehand and backhand volleys lead the racket slightly with the butt. This will create some underspin on the ball which will help with control and direction.

**OPPONENT AIMING RIGHT AT YOU?** This often happens, in doubles particularly. The self-defence shot is always the backhand.

Sometimes it is good to be on tip-toes to play a high volley — it adds aggression.

**TURNING DEFENCE INTO ATTACK:** Should you make a good defensive lob and you see your opponent chasing back for it, approach the net stealthily. This tactic aims to finish off the rally with a good volley on the next shot.

**THE DIFFICULT LOW VOLLEY:** Most players have some difficulty with this shot. Simply remember: deep knee bend, your head should be low with the racket head, slightly tilt the racket head in order to elevate the ball over the net, squeeze the grip while imparting some underspin for control.

**PRACTICES FOR CLASSICAL VOLLEYS**

a Position yourself inside the service box. Have your practice partner serve into the box. Return their serves with volleys. This is not easy to do, but it will improve your handling of difficult volleys.

b Let your practice partner feed you with volleys as they call out simultaneously which type of volley they would like you to play, e.g., short, deep, angled, etc. This type of practice will help to quicken your reaction and feel for different types of volleys.

**SWING VOLLEYS OR DRIVE VOLLEYS**

a This is usually the volley to use if you are caught mid-court.

**b** Some players have difficulty ending the point with a classical volley.

**c** The swing volley should be hit at shoulder level, even more in front of the body than the classical. The follow-through should finish all the way to the other shoulder. The key to this shot is to start your run for the ball early enough, in order to be able to pick it out of the air at shoulder level i.e., before the ball starts to drop.

**d** The swing volley is very popular today among better players. It needs practice to build up confidence to use it in match play.

**THE VOLLEY AS FINISHING SHOT:** When you are in a good position to hit either a classical or swing volley, try to end the point at your first attempt. You might get passed on the next!

# Tips to
# Improve
# your Overhead

## POSITIONING

**a** The key to a successful overhead lies in good footwork. Always use small adjusting steps.

**b** Try and place yourself well under the ball. This begins with a well-timed shoulder turn.

**SIGHTING THE BALL:** The spare hand should point to the oncoming ball and stay up in order to secure a good position. To do this correctly, keep your head up high and your eyes glued to the oncoming ball.

**PREPARATION:** Good preparation for an overhead is similar to the posture of an archer pulling at their bow and getting ready to release an arrow.

**PLACEMENT:** Placement of an overhead is usually more important than power.

**POWER:** However sometimes it is necessary to hit the ball with 100 percent full strength in order to bounce it well over the head of the opposition!

**SLICED OVERHEAD:** The sliced overhead with spin on the ball is usually played from the deuce court into the opponent's deuce court (for right-handed players). This is a particularly useful shot in doubles.

**DEALING WITH A DEEP LOB:** If you're receiving a deep lob beyond the service line it is often wise to let it bounce. This is important simply to check that it is in court. You can still play a smash once the ball has bounced. Once again, positioning using adjustable little steps is of critical importance.

**DEALING WITH A SHALLOW LOB:** If the lob is short, say *inside* the serve line, it is best to take time away from the opponent and play it in the air.

**LATE GETTING INTO POSITION:** Should you be late with the take back, hit the ball with an extended hand, without bending your elbow. This is also known as a bowling action.

**THE BACKHAND OVERHEAD:** This is probably the most difficult shot in tennis. Try to avoid it if possible, as not much power or control can be generated from this position. Best to move around the ball and position yourself on the other side so that you can take it in the normal way.

The best way to practice this shot is with a partner. Your partner could be practicing their lobs getting deeper and deeper, while you are working on your overhead. Then swap roles.

**PRACTICING THE OVERHEAD WITHOUT A PARTNER:** Practice against a wall. Hitting down into the base of the wall produces a high ball for your next smash and so on.

**THE IMPORTANCE OF A GOOD OVERHEAD:** A well hit overhead always gives confidence and motivation. Conversely, the inability to put the ball away brings with it anxiety. It is worthwhile working on your overhead as a valuable match tool.

# Tips to
# Improve your
# Mentality and Tactics

Sit or lie down comfortably where you will not be disturbed. Take three deep breaths exhaling through your nose. This is always the best start toward solving any mental problem.

## RESURRECTING THAT SELF-CONFIDENT FEELING
a Remember clearly how you felt unbeatable and full of confidence before a match.

b The time to recapture that feeling is 15–20 minutes before the next match. Close your eyes. Relax and imagine you are playing faultless tennis because the ball is the size of a football and you simply cannot miss. Now think about your game plan and apply it to your imagination.

c When you start to crystalize your thinking make sure you are on your own. Imagine the racket is in your hand and the tennis court under your feet, all the time thinking about how it felt when you were last confident. Try to replicate that feeling. Physically feel that confidence move slowly throughout your body. Think your deepest thoughts and say them out loud! (See Tip 179.) Listen to your breathing. Try to breathe calmly, emulating the way you breathed when you were last confident.

d When you feel mentally engaged, pump your fist and be happy that you have found your confidence within yourself.

**USE OF MANTRA:** Continue holding your fist pumped and repeat your special mantra three times, helping you to sustain that very special self-confident feeling. Now say out loud "Let's go!" or "You can do it!", "Come on!" or simply "Now!" Then open your fist and concentrate on your breathing. Repeat this ritual four to six times until you feel it is working for you. Simply repeat the process when required.

**THE POWER OF A SMILE:** To smile on court is not forbidden! In fact quite the reverse. Smiling helps to de-tensify not only your face but your whole body.

**THE POWER OF THE SCORE:** The score can affect any player. If they lead then there is pressure to close the match out. If they are losing, they might fear they are nearing the end of the match and start to play without heart. So always try to focus on the very next point whatever the score.

**OPPONENTS**
a An over-confident opponent (otherwise known as cocky!) can easily lose their focus and intensity. So be ready to grab any opportunity they present you with.

b Should your opponent be in a hurry to wipe you off the court, try to play a few unpredictable shots in order to surprise them. Let the opponent know that you are still alive and trying.

c Sometimes an opponent can seem disinterested. Don't let that put you off. Learn to keep your focus at all times and don't let up.

ATTRACTING ATTENTION: Ask yourself seriously whether you wish to win or only to attract attention by the use of eye-catching, risky shot-making. If you are serious about winning, you need to find a winning game against every type of opponent.

GETTING IN THE ZONE
a Before a match try listening to music to relax you.

b Think about the match, imagining your opponent and how they may respond.

**GAME PLAN:** Set appropriate game plans for all future matches, incorporating technical, tactical and psychological aspects. For example, tell yourself "do not hit the ball too often up the middle of the court" or "try to get more out of the opponent's second serve by speeding up your racket acceleration when returning their second serve." Some players like to write these ideas down in note form and take them on the court in their tennis bag so that they can remind themselves at change-overs or during rain delays (along with this book of course!).

**THE VALUE OF QUALITY STROKES:** Even the best tactics in the world will not help you win a match unless you possess the quality strokes to begin with. So make sure your ground strokes and serve are as sound and reliable as they can be.

**OPPONENTS' STRENGTHS AND WEAKNESSES**
a As soon as possible try to ascertain opponents' strengths and weaknesses — if not before the match by scouting, then certainly in the warm up.

b In general, it makes sense to try to play away from opponents' strengths.

c Should you discover an opponent's striking weakness then make a point of exposing it only on important points for your advantage, such as 30–40, or 40–30 and particularly on game set r m pc ts.

d Be warned that if you constantly pick on opponents' weaknesses during the match, they are able to practice that shot to their advantage and may eventually become more proficient and confident.

**SELF IMPROVEMENT:** Use every match to try and improve. Try to recognize your weaknesses quickly and work on them in practice until they become weapons. The will to win is worthless without the will to practice!

**NEW MATCHES:** Treat every new match as another opportunity. It is essential to use practice time in between matches to try and correct what you know let you down previously.

**NO EXCUSES:** Excuses like "my opponent cheated," "he pushed the ball" or "it was too windy" all help to expose a weak mentality on your part.

**ATTITUDE:** Be positive every time you walk off court in the knowledge that you have given 100 percent effort. You should not have to explain yourself to anyone.

**SOLID PLAYERS:** When players improve their footwork and stop making unforced errors they are referred to as "solid" players. The next step is to learn how to place the ball where you want it. Then practice this control every day using targets to improve accuracy.

## AVOID NEGATIVE THOUGHTS:
Try to avoid thinking "what will happen if I make a mistake here?" or "how could I miss that shot?" Instead give yourself an objective for the next point. For example, think about the placement of your next serve or return of serve, or the type of serve you are now going to use.

## USE OF KEY WORDS:
When you're faced with important points try to stay calm by using your key phrases like "just return the serve!" or "first serve in!" or "step into the ball!" etc.

## 90-SECOND CHANGEOVERS
a Control your emotions by keeping your mind on the court and the job in hand. Don't allow either your eyes or your thoughts to wander. Keep your eyes firmly on the ground or on your racket strings. It is also a good time to close your eyes for a short while, while you plan and visualize your next moves.

b Take the time to check out your racket strings to make sure they are properly aligned. Dry yourself with a towel. Even if it is not very hot this is the time to wrap your head and neck with a cold, wet towel or ice. This will help you feel less tired.

## PLAYING DIFFICULT OR EXPERIENCED OPPONENTS

a When playing an experienced opponent your first chance to turn the match around may be your last, so grab the opportunity!

b In a critical phase of the match, after losing an important point, keep calm and try to focus on the next point. A few deep breaths will help, concentrating on exhaling, not inhaling.

c Throwing the racket and getting visibly upset is a welcome sight for any opponent.

d On the other hand opponents notice when you fight hard and stay positive after losing a point. It tells them you are no easy push-over.

## IDEAS TO IMPROVE

a List all your necessary improvements for future matches and make them your short-term goals.

b If possible, record your match. When viewing it back later, stop at every important point and list your good and bad play. Next time you go to practice, take that list with you You will know automatically how to proceed.

c Note how you won points during your previous matches and use that information. Learn to apply these particular shots as weapons at critical times in future.

d Recognize what led to your frustration during the match. Was it the wind? Bad calls? In your next match learn to overcome this by focusing on that one element only.

e Frustrated players tend to rush following a few mistakes. They then make more mistakes. Smart opponents, having recognized this, encourage their frustrated opponent to lose the match even quicker by staying particularly calm. This is even more irritating to a frustrated opponent!

f The first two points in each game are particularly important. By making an extra effort to win those regularly, you will automatically put pressure on your opponent to have to come from behind all the time.

## DEALING WITH DEFEAT

a Do not grieve too long after a defeat. It could affect your next match. Rather, learn from your losses.

b It is smart to wait at least one hour after finishing a match before you start to analyze it with either your coach or parent. You should be in a more receptive mood by then and will hopefully have emotionally calmed down.

c When you finally make a start on the analysis, always begin with your own assessment of what transpired on the court.

d If you have to do this sort of analysis on your own, learn to be brutally honest. It is an absolute waste of time to kid yourself.

It is always recommended to give a good firm handshake following every match — win or lose!

## DEALING WITH WINNING

a Naturally this creates a much better atmosphere in which to receive both criticism and suggestions on how to improve even more!

b Statistics should still be made of your winners, unforced errors, winning serves and winning attacks to the net (if any); these should be discussed in great detail.

c Even when they're winning, some players have difficulty in successfully finishing off a match. Don't rush. Unforced errors will only start to appear.

d When you're winning, never play too safe. Never lose your creativity. Continue to go after your shots while focusing on staying calm.

## PSYCHOLOGICAL LAPSE IN MATCH PLAY:
If you experience this, as most players do from time to time, instead of resting, you should perform easy disciplines and drills in practice in order to try and regain your confidence.

## LOSING MATCHES AFTER BEING CLOSE TO WINNING:
These are the most frustrating types of match to lose. If it happens several times in a row try and rebuild your self-confidence by playing less strong

opposition for a short while. Then, as your self-confidence slowly starts to build, quality opponents can be reinstated gradually.

**ELIMINATE NEGATIVE THINKING:** Never think "now, don't make a mistake here." Focus instead on the next point and what you are going to do to win it.

**BEHAVIOR:** By always exhibiting fair sportsmanship both on and off court, your behavior will naturally encourage spectators, umpires and referees to be on your side. This will be really helpful when a serious conflict arises.

### WEATHER CONDITIONS
**a** Try and make weather conditions your ally. This can be an advantage when you're up against an opponent who dislikes excessive wind or sun, or perhaps a little dampness.

**b** The way to do this is to not restrict all of your practice to indoors. Make a point of practicing some of the time on outside courts, where the elements come into play. If you do this you can figure out how best to use the elements to your advantage.

Keeping an eye on the weather at Wimbledon:
rain breaks can be used to your advantage.

**CATCHING UP IN A MATCH:** When you are gaining ground on an opponent who had a significant lead on you, never allow a wrong call either by your opponent or the umpire to throw you off. Never cause a fuss as this is the surest way to lose your focus. Instead, make a point of staying positive and continue your attack.

Losing? One spectacular point — or even one really good shot — can give you the impetus to turn a match around. If you're losing, try to occasionally play outside your normal range and see if it works for you.

## PLAYING "PUSHERS"

**a** These are players who are well known for retrieving many balls and who are extremely consistent. They do a lot of winning, but at the same time they are limited — the reason being they can only win within range of their own level.

**b** When your opponent only rallies deep balls without much pace recognize that you are playing a pusher. Their style seldom changes so you have to be very disciplined when playing them.

**c** It is essential when playing pushers *not* to attempt to go for winners on every stroke, even if their consistent style drives you crazy! It is better to move them around and wait for the shorter ball, then hit an approach shot and come to the net.

d Because of their style of play pushers will encourage you to aim for the lines, so that you make more mistakes than usual. Only go for clean winners when you have created an obvious opportunity. Then increase your pace and really lean into the ball.

e Pushers naturally have good footwork. For that reason it is advantageous to mix up your pace and ball placements. Try to wrong foot them and this will neutralize their foot speed.

f Without losing your consistency try to slowly take control of the points. Do not allow the occasional lob or passing shot to upset you. It is also ok to play deep, and advance to the net occasionally to add variety. Pushers usually don't have the sharp angles to pass you. As a result they will have to come up with some new shot which is not to their liking or their strength.

g When playing this type of player anticipate some slow and high-bouncing balls. Occasionally you could surprise them by hitting a high-bouncing and deep ball yourself, followed by sneaking into the net when they are preoccupied by moving backward. After such a strategy, particularly if it proves successful, they will be unsure of your intentions in the future and likely become confused.

h Most pushers have fairly weak serves, particularly their second serves. This presents an excellent opportunity to keep pressure on them — constantly attack their serve!

i Their net-play usually also lacks quality, so play short balls and low cross-court. You must try to move them from their comfort zone on the baseline and make them hit the shots they dislike, such as volleys, overheads, and most shots from inside the court.

j When you think you have hit a winner, anticipate one more shot from the pusher — this is always their strength.

k Keep trying to control each and every point with your strengths. Never give way to their neutral type of game.

SAVING MATCH-POINT: If the match is nearing its end and your opponent has a match-point against you, this is their chance. However, it can be yours too! By putting in a major effort to win that one point, or maybe the entire game, the momentum can swing, and you now have a good chance to win the entire match. Saving match-points can often re-ignite your motivation while having the opposite effect on your opponent.

**PERIODIZATION:** For serious competitive players, it is essential *not to play* at regular intervals throughout the year. In order to recharge your batteries make sure you take a few days off every couple of months. Without these necessary rest periods, you are much more prone to injury and staleness. So when you're planning your program for the year, don't forget to include essential rest periods.

**EXHAUSTED?** Feeling tired is usually more mental than physical. If you ever feel exhausted on court, just remember that you probably still have something like half a tank remaining!

## LOVE THE CHALLENGE!

a To be a top-class "pro" player you have to start off with a love of playing all sorts of matches. Funnily enough it is as important to play weaker players regularly, as it is to play stronger ones. It is only against the weaker players that you can try out all your new shots and sequences, slowly adding them to your repertoire. So here are a few suggestions you might look to play on a regular basis in order to compile as valuable and varied a program as possible.

b Play against top-club amateurs, play against "cheaters" with as large an audience as possible, play when it is sunny, when it is windy, late at night when the light is fading, and of course under lights both indoors and out. Sometimes it is a valuable stin lant t ave a small bet on a practice game — although one h itates to mention that these days — because it does increase the pressure. However, the main objective is to play as many matches as possible.

c To be conscious of your breathing is important since it is also an extra bonus for improving your concentration. Breathe through your nose, *not* your mouth. If you're facing critical situations in matches, listening to your breathing can help to de-stress you, which in turn keeps your mind off being nervous — a valuable tool.

d In order to improve the quality of your play and control nervousness even further, it is important to exhale as you go into your shots. This is not a loud noise or grunt, as is often heard, but simply a positive release of breath. Many players subconsciously hold their breath throughout the entire rally through sheer anxiety. The simple "letting go" of the breath adds dividends to your effort and stamina throughout.

PERFORMING RITUALS: This enhances your concentration and keeps it where it is best — on the court. For example, just before serving, pause, then bounce the ball a few times to help bring you into the zone. If on the other hand it is your turn to return serve, then again pause first, then stimulate your feet by bouncing up and down.

Carrying your racket in your non-dominant hand in between points helps to release the tension in your playing arm. Also make sure the head of your racket is *up* and not dangling down — a much better form of body language!

**20 SECONDS BETWEEN POINTS:** Don't waste this valuable time as you walk around the court. You can shelter in the shadows at the back of the court or simply walk to where you are supposed to be. Whatever you decide, walk slowly and keep your eyes firmly fixed downwards while you think what to do next. Checking out the audience or rushing from side to side without thinking is certainly not advised!

Posture — an important give-away! Always walk tall in a relaxed fashion. Make sure your shoulders are well back and loose. Shake them occasionally to de-tensify.

**EMOTIONAL CONTROL:** Matches are frequently lost, very often from winning positions, by players losing their cool. Practice ignoring all the irritating factors in matches that are of no real importance, and at least always try to *look* cool.

Friendly with the opponent? If you are really serious about winning, seasoned competitive players will tell you it doesn't pay to become too friendly with any opponent.

**SHAKING HANDS:** Nevertheless, should you lose a match, be sure to give your opponent a firm handshake. At the same time, be an actor, and force a smile! It costs nothing, but simultaneously you might say to yourself, "Now I know your game, I'll beat the hell out of you next time!"

**THE IMPORTANCE OF WRITING NOTES:** Don't be afraid to write down your thoughts on paper. Write anything and everything, both good and bad, on all your matches, practices, and opponents. This all helps to reinforce your discipline and your decisions — and tennis is all about discipline and decisions!

# Tips to
# Improve your Doubles Play

**FIRST SERVE IN:** In doubles it is not as important to serve hard as it is to maintain a high percentage of first serves in (aim for at least 75 percent).

**SERVING DOWN THE CENTER LINE:** Your serve should be deep, with lots of elevation, spin and good placement. Keeping the serve down the center line most of the time is preferable. This helps to cut off the angles on both sides.

**KEEP RETURNS LOW OVER THE NET:** Most returns should be low and away from the net opponent.

**BE READY TO ATTACK SECOND SERVES:** When possible attack the opponent's second serve, move forward and close in on the court.

**LOBBING IS VALUABLE:** Topspin lobs, whether offensive or defensive, are some of the most valuable shots in tennis. However, too much lobbing usually results in the eventual loss of the match. Therefore avoid taking too much of a defensive role.

## DOUBLES OFFERS MORE COURT — USE IT!

As you have probably gathered by now, playing doubles teaches you much more about the game than singles, because it is more tactical. There is also more court in which to play. So learn to use the extra width offered in the alleys.

## PRACTICE HALF-VOLLEYS: Half-volleys are the most difficult shots to play. However they appear often in doubles. So special practice to perfect the extra timing and bending necessary for half-volleys is recommended.

## UP AGAINST TWO GOOD VOLLEYERS? If you find you are up against two very good net players, it may be advisable to stay on the base-line and start aiming for successful passing shots.

## AUSTRALIAN FORMATION: This is used by the serving team to block a good cross-court return of serve. When this is applied the server's partner stands on the same side as the server. As players are allowed to stand anywhere, both take up a central position, one almost behind the other. The server aims for a down-the-line serve in order to minimize the angled return. However in order not to hit their partner at the net, it is best for the server's partner to crouch down, kneel or do both. Lastly the serving team need to agree who will cover the exposed side-line and alley once the return is struck by their opponents. Whatever they decide, the net player on the serving team needs to be particularly active. They need to intercept as many balls as possible, almost to the distraction of the opposition.

## COMMUNICATION/SIGNALS:

1 Never look at your partner when they are serving.

2 Instead learn to continually look at your opponents, trying all the time to pick up clues about where and how they may be planning to return.

3 Constant communication and mutual support is the key to a successful doubles team, particularly in the Australian formation. Devise signals and practice them continually to avoid any confusion in match-play. It is a good investment to spend time both on and off the court with your doubles partner.

Keeping parallel with your partner is one doubles strategy that often works well. Venus and Serena Williams very often play this way.

# Tips to
# Improve your
# Fitness and Nutrition

**BOXING:** With the assistance of your coach or trainer, do 20 minutes of boxing training regularly. Punch a bag or your coach's boxing gloves. Boxers tend not to have lower back, shoulder, or stomach injuries because these muscle groups are well conditioned.

**DYNABAND TRAINING:** A Dynaband is a long piece of thick rectangular rubber used for resistance exercises. Tie the Dynaband around your waist. While your coach holds one end behind you, resist the band and run forward 8 to 11 yards (7–10 meters) for five repetitions.

**JUMPING ROPE:** This is good for a short warm-up. Jumping with both knees up at the same time is the best type of skipping for agility. Short sharp bursts of about 20 at a time are best, done repeatedly with rest periods of about 20 seconds between each, simulating the rest periods between points in a match.

**MEDICINE BALL:** Two to three times a week practice holding a heavy medicine ball with both hands, simulating the forehand and backhand drive motions. Do three sets of 10 repetitions by throwing it down the line and cross-court.

Throw the medicine ball straight up into the air as high as possible 10 times for two sets. Then throw the ball, either to a partner or against a wall, starting above your head with both hands for two sets of 10 repetitions.

**DUMBBELLS:** Take a dumbbell in each hand. Lower yourself by stepping forward and then backward with each leg. Which weight you use should depend on your physical ability and level of fitness.

**SHORT SPRINTS:** Run short sprints on the tennis court in all directions, touching each line separately with your hand — this means bending, simulating tennis movements.

**FOOTWORK AND ENDURANCE:** Try to keep a rally going for as long as possible with your playing partner or coach. In order to increase the intensity and enjoyment of this exercise, each player should count out loud as the ball is struck. When this becomes too easy, repeat the same exercise but using only the areas between the service-line and base-line.

**USING YOUR NON-DOMINANT HAND:** Make a point of practicing with the racket in your non-dominant hand once a week, and once a month try to play a set with this hand. If you're two-handed adjust your grip and move your hand position. Ok, it might not be easy, but this all makes you more adaptable and flexible as a player.

**STRETCHING:** To get your muscles warmed up and ready to play remember to do some active stretching before a practice or match; for example, use the active hamstring and external rotators stretches shown (see Figures 2 and 3). These stretches are only effective if you break into a sweat. Half-hearted stretching is no use at all!

Figure 2: Active hamstring stretch

Figure 3: External rotators stretch

**WARM-UP:** Use your warm up to try out all your shots and play three to four gentle games.

**POST-PLAY STRETCHING:** Following a match or practice you need to do some gentle, cool-down stretching.

## IMPROVING BALANCE:

a Try playing occasionally in a pair of old socks instead of trainers, or play mini-tennis barefoot. Because the grip of the shoes is missing, the muscles in the feet and legs must work more, in turn enhancing balance.

b Assume the position as if you were just about to return a blistering serve — a "return the serve swing" — and hold it for a minute.

c Do the same with the serve and the volley and hold them for 20–30 seconds. Repeat three times with a 30-second pause between each.

d Stand on one foot and keep your balance at the same time as touching the ground, first in front of you, then behind, and lastly next to you, always returning to the starting position (feet slightly apart with hands loosely at sides) between each pose. The other hand should be extended above your head. When this exercise becomes routine, take a light dumbbell and hold it in the hand that touches the ground.

## IMPROVING EXPLOSIVENESS: Jump as high as you can, with both feet stretched out in front of you if possible. Extend both hands toward your toes as you jump. Repeat 10 times.

## STRENGTHENING YOUR ABDOMINALS: Lying on your back on a stability ball, with your feet firmly on the ground, raise your upper body slowly. Keep your neck and thighs relaxed to make sure it is your abdominals that do the work. Your hands should be resting on your chest. Do three sets of 15 repetitions.

**PROTECTING YOUR LOWER BACK:** To strengthen your back muscles and improve your balance at the same time, stand with your back to a wall, with a stability ball between you and the wall. Bend your knees slowly and lower yourself. Do not allow the ball to drop until the exercise is completed. It's harder than it sounds! Build up your repetitions gradually, starting with only three. The same exercise can be done using dumbbells in each hand or while standing on one leg!

**BALANCE:** Do ballet exercises, standing on one leg at a time. With one foot firmly on the ground, raise and bend the other leg, drawing circles in the air with the knee, first one way and then the other. Repeat with the other leg.

**BALANCE:** Standing on one leg, point the raised toe forward, then to 45 degrees, then to 90 degrees. Repeat to either side with each leg.

**TENNIS-RELATED MUSCLE GROUPS:** Build up your muscles in the gym — ideally scheduling two to three visits a week. Explore your weaknesses with a qualified fitness trainer and create a program to improve your strength and power.

**PRESERVATION OF ROTATOR CUFF:** The rotator cuff is the group of muscles that stabilizes the shoulder and which endures enormous strain during tennis matches. Remember to use a Dynaband (resistance band) to strengthen these muscles regularly. Most professional players carry at least one with them whenever they are on the road.

ABDOMINAL AND LOWER BACK MUSCLES:
Lower back injuries are one of the most common injuries in tennis. So learn to strengthen and stretch both your abdominal and back muscles *before* injuries occur.

RESTING AND REHABILITATION: Take resting seriously — if you're injured and you take it slow you can return to form more quickly and more efficiently. Don't try to return to play too soon.

MASSAGE/STRETCHING/SAUNA/JACUZZI:
Don't underestimate the value of regular massages and a good stretching program, plus the regular use of a sauna and jacuzzi. They can be as important as your stroke training and fitness preparation, as they may help to keep the muscles relaxed and in better shape while they are recovering.

FITNESS TRAINER: Every serious tennis player should have a personal fitness trainer whose job it is to supervise and prepare a fitness program. It should be individually tailored to you based on your age, tournament schedule, ambitions and previous injuries.

**INJURY PRACTICE:** Never miss a practice, even if you are injured. If your arm hurts you can try to keep moving by practicing footwork that day. But remember to take it easy.

**MAKE A SPLASH!** If you have a leg injury, get in the pool and use an old racket to simulate the strokes while standing in the water.

Practicing strokes in the pool is a good way to remain active, despite a leg injury.

**SPORTS SUPPLEMENTS:** Visit a sports nutritionist to find out what vitamins and minerals should be added to your diet. Particularly important are antioxidants, like vitamins E, C, B6 and B12. Selenium and zinc are also important, but be sure to follow the recommended dosage. Taking more than the recommended dose puts extra strain on your body and can be counterproductive.

**WHEN AND WHAT TO EAT:** You should eat two to three hours before a match or practice. This meal should be rich in carbohydrates such as pasta, rice, bread or potatoes — try a baked potato with chives and beans, chicken and rice, pasta with pesto or sandwiches with natural peanut butter. Before practice all these foods will help you to take on the carbohydrates and energy you will need. Drink water to make sure you are fully hydrated too.

**TAKE IN!** Eat a diet rich in fish, chicken, brown pasta, brown rice, honey, wholemeal or wholegrain bread, fresh fruits and vegetables.

**SEND BACK!** Cut down on, or eliminate from your diet, pork, beef, all processed meat like ham, sausages and paté, fatty meat, animal fats (cheese, butter, cream), chocolate and white bread.

**HYDRATION:** During competition be sure to hydrate yourself properly. The best way is to prepare your own sports drink, made from selected supplements, proteins, carbohydrates and vitamins. A sports dietician can advise you on this, or commercial sports drinks are available. Check the ingredients carefully.

**WHEN TO DRINK:** Be sure to drink plenty of water *before*, *during* and *after* exercise. About 5 to 7 oz (150–200ml) every 15–20 minutes is perfect, except during play when your uptake should be slower to prevent bloating or unwanted washroom breaks. If you feel thirsty, it is too late and you are already dehydrated! Water needs to be between 46 and 53° F (8–12° C) unless the player has already adapted to colder water.

**WHEN TO EAT AND DRINK FOLLOWING A MATCH:** Within 30 minutes of coming off court, snack on some fruit or fruit drinks as these are gentle on an empty stomach. Within an hour you need to eat a good meal containing protein, carbohydrates and vegetables to aid recovery, e.g., a piece of chicken (skin removed) with steamed vegetables and basmati rice, or a piece of fish with a baked potato and green beans. Then four hours after this, have a large protein meal. Remember to stock up on fruit and fruit drinks again.

**WHAT NOT TO DRINK:** Avoid all carbonated drinks as the sodium (salt) content can cause muscle cramps.

**WEIGHT CONTROL:** Work out your natural playing weight with a sports nutritionist and remember that it is really important to maintain that weight. Carrying excess weight around the court will only slow you down!

**HEAT AND SUN:** Always protect yourself from the sun. Wear a hat and light-colored clothes — white is best as darker clothes attract the heat more. Use your game breaks to maximize your time in the shade. Wet or damp clothes should be changed immediately. At change-overs cool yourself by placing ice or a cold, wet towel on your back, head and neck. Always use sunscreen and don't forget to top up with water (see Tip 296).

**HANG TIME:** Hanging stretches everything! A few moments with your feet off the ground, allowing all your weight to fall, held by straight arms from a bar or a rope-ladder (like the ones found in children's playgrounds), helps to maintain a healthy back.

**THE BENEFITS OF YOGA:** Yoga loosens stiffening joints and muscles and releases any tension — it's great for body and mind. Join a local class and use what you learn there at home. Before a big match, especially if you can't sleep, working through some relaxing stretches is certainly healthier than taking sleeping pills!

**THE VALUE OF SLEEP AND REST:** In order to perform anywhere near your best the following day you need to get eight hours of sleep — sometimes more, never less. Sleep is so critical, and a lack of it can affect your decision-making; it controls your weight (when you're tired you tend to eat more) and it impacts your memory. Sleep is as important as diet to help guarantee your peak perform-ance. If you can't sleep, even resting with your feet up watching TV, reading or watching a video of tomorrow's opponent will be more beneficial than late-night socializing — as many top players have discovered to their cost.

And one final tip — the most important one of all . . .
*Re-read this booklet again and again, and always keep it in your tennis bag!*